AF381487

DEVELOPING YOUR ASSERTIVENESS

Communicate clearly and improve your professional relationships

Written by Véronique Bronckart
Translated by Rebecca Neal

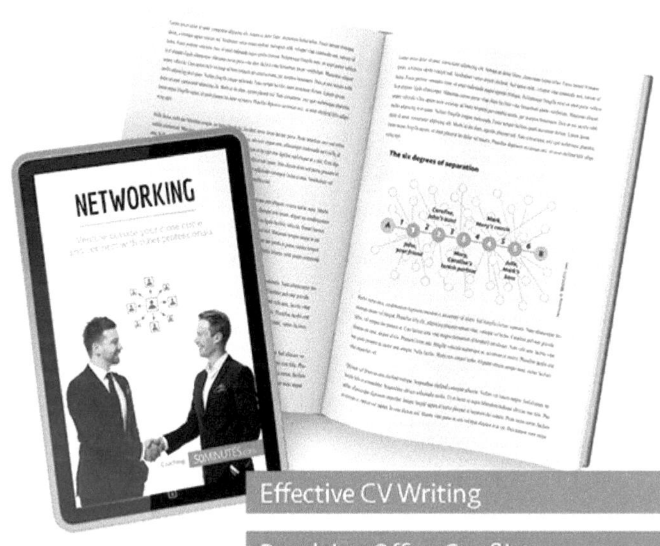

NETWORKING

DEVELOPING YOUR ASSERTIVENESS

- **Problem:** how can you communicate your point of view and needs while respecting other people's opinions and boundaries?
- **Uses:** standing up for yourself without coming across as arrogant or aggressive contributes to effective, healthy communication at work.
- **Professional context:** professional relationships, personal development, social psychology, management, conflict resolution.
- **FAQs:**
  - What is assertiveness?
  - In what situations can assertiveness help me?
  - How can I be assertive without coming across as aggressive or arrogant?
  - What is the difference between assertiveness and selfishness?
  - How can I change my behaviour to become more assertive?
  - What impact can assertiveness have on my

professional life?

In both our professional and personal lives, we are often bombarded with requests and demands that are overly persistent or that seem unreasonable to us. However, all too often we do not dare to say no, either because we are afraid of disappointing the other person or because we want to avoid conflict, even though the situation leaves us feeling frustrated, upset or angry. Understandably, many of us want to learn how to avoid these kinds of situations, how to avoid simply going along with what other people ask of us, how to assert ourselves without causing conflict or disappointment, and how to stand up for ourselves without hurting other people.

There is only one solution: assertiveness. Assertiveness is often confused with arrogance or aggression, but there is a big difference between these attitudes. While the aim of aggression is to hurt other people and arrogance implies a degree of contempt for others, assertiveness is about respecting yourself and those around you. However, the boundary between these different attitudes is sometimes blurred, and it is easy to come across as threatening rather than considerate. This means that effective communication is vital, and in order to achieve this you need to be self-aware and in tune with your own needs and values.

If you struggle to put forward an argument, say no or speak up in meetings, either when dealing with your colleagues or when talking to your manager, this guide is for you. In 50 minutes, you will discover a series of key steps, tips and exercises that will enable you to develop your assertiveness.

DEVELOPING YOUR ASSERTIVENESS: THE BASICS

WHAT IS ASSERTIVENESS?

Assertiveness refers to our capacity to express ourselves and defend our rights and opinions while also respecting the rights and opinions of others. Behaving assertively means stating our needs, emotions, boundaries and beliefs clearly, confidently and honestly, without hurting the other person.

Unfortunately, even though the aim of assertiveness is to guarantee mutual respect and avoid harming others, miscommunications and misunderstandings mean that it is often taken for aggression or arrogance. The table below illustrates different kinds of behaviour in a professional setting in order to give you a better understanding of this concept:

The different kinds of behaviour at work

AVOIDANCE
Defensive approach. Does not provide a solution and simply puts the problem off until later.
PASSIVITY
Compliant approach which has some similarities with avoidance and generally stems from an inability to express oneself due to a lack of self-confidence. This can result in self-effacement.
ASSERTIVENESS
Considerate approach based on self-respect and respect for other people which requires direct, honest and appropriate communication. This behaviour contributes to effective, healthy professional relationships.
MANIPULATION
Dominating approach which involves using cunning to steer another person's behaviour and thoughts. Manipulators aim to get what they want by any means possible, even if this risks creating conflict. This behaviour signals a lack of respect for others.

<table>
<tr><td align="center">AGGRESSION</td></tr>
<tr><td>Offensive approach with the aim of harming others, with very negative consequences. This hurtful behaviour has no positive results and can lead to rejection by others.</td></tr>
</table>

HOW CAN ASSERTIVENESS HELP YOU AT WORK?

Assertiveness plays an important role in professional relationships and in management:

- your professional relationships will improve and become healthier thanks to the clear, honest expression of both parties' needs;
- you will develop your interpersonal intelligence, meaning your ability to adapt how you communicate based on the situation and the person you are talking to;
- you will make your colleagues feel more comfortable and at ease;
- you will be more likely to get results from negotiations and secure deals;
- you will be less stressed and your risk of burnout will be lower, because you will be able to politely say no to your colleagues when you

have too much to do;
- your confidence and your team's trust in you will increase when you engage with your responsibilities and take firmer stances;
- you will learn how to deliver constructive criticism with the aim of changing other people's actions and behaviour in order to reach your objectives;
- you will remain honest with yourself and respect your needs and the needs of other people, which will allow you to avoid power plays and manipulation;
- finally, your overall wellbeing will improve.

BENEFITS FOR THE ENTIRE COMPANY

If just one or two people develop this positive behaviour, the overall atmosphere in the company will improve. Exchanges between departments and meetings will become more efficient because communication will be more effective. Objectives will be more precisely defined and each person's role and contribution will be more clearly identified, which may in turn reduce sources of conflict. However, the opposite is equally true: treating your colleagues poorly will encourage them to behave in the same way. Think about your own wellbeing and the wellbeing of your team, and act accordingly.

HOW CAN YOU FIND THE COURAGE TO EXPRESS YOURSELF?

The first step in gaining the courage to express yourself is to understand yourself, respect your feelings and needs, gain control of your emotions and be clear about your expectations, while minimising any unpleasantness for the other person. This may seem complicated, so we have put together the diagram below to make things easier for you.

The steps to assertiveness

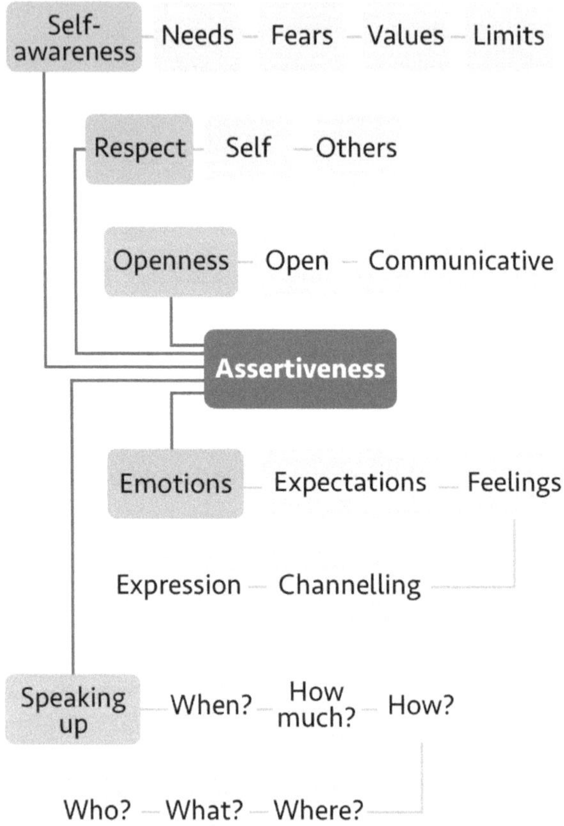

Self-awareness

The first step towards assertiveness is to understand and accept your needs, fears, values and limits. To identify these, ask yourself: "What do I need? What is important to me? What drives me? What am I afraid of? Why does this situation bother me? How does this situation make me feel? What are my limits?" These questions will allow you to identify what is and is not essential for you. Asserting yourself and arguing over every subject will get you nowhere, so focus on the things that really matter to you.

THREE KINDS OF LIMITS

There are different kind of limits. Specifically, limits can be linked to:

- **What is possible and impossible.** This involves distinguishing between what is genuinely feasible and what is not. For example, sending an email will be impossible if you have no internet connection.
- **Rules and norms.** This involves actions and behaviours which do not respect the rules. These rules can be formally written

down as regulations or laws, or can be linked to manners and etiquette. For example, smoking during a meeting would be frowned upon.

- **Your values, beliefs and needs.** These limits emerge when you feel frustrated, uncomfortable or angry at the things you are being asked to do, because they are not in line with your values and beliefs, or because they prevent you from fulfilling your own needs. These kinds of limits are generally the ones standing in the way of developing your assertiveness. Imagine that your colleague asks you to alter a figure in an accounting document to cover up a mistake they have made: not only is this against the rules, but it also goes against one of your values, honesty. Another situation could be that your boss asks you to work late to finalise a report, but you have been invited out for a meal for your friend's birthday. This bothers you because you need to be free tonight.

Respect for yourself and for other people

As we have already explained, assertiveness is based on respect for yourself and other people. To respect yourself, you need to be able to communicate with yourself. This does not mean talking to yourself, but rather understanding and accepting who you are (your personality), what you are (your behaviour and actions), what you can do (your skills and abilities) and what matters to you (your values, desires and needs). You will then be able to act in keeping with who you really are and avoid sources of frustration, discomfort and stress. We can illustrate this with an example: one of your colleagues asks you to help them finish a report. This bothers you because if you accept, you will end up falling behind, and being up to date with your work is important to you. This means that helping out your colleague – which would show that you care about and respect them – would be detrimental to your own wellbeing. However, this does not mean that you should just say no to everything you are asked without listening to the other person! Instead, you should be respectful towards both sides by analysing each person's needs and trying to find a compromise. In our example, a good approach would be to explain to your colleague that you have an urgent task to finish, but that you will help them as soon as you are done. This solution demonstrates three different forms of respect:

Forms of respect

I respect you	"You know that I'm always happy to help you."
I respect myself	"I'll do it once my urgent task is finished."
Respect me	"If you'd told me early, I'd have been able to plan around it."

You can make sure that you are respecting your own principles and those of the other person by using the life positions set out in transactional analysis, which is a tool for identifying, understanding and analysing interpersonal relationships. Life positions were developed by the Canadian-born psychiatrist Eric Berne (1910-1970) and are used to represent the value we assign to ourselves and other people. Positive views of ourselves, other people and the world ("OK", represented by a plus sign) are distingui-shed from negative views ("not OK", represented by a minus sign). In this way, Berne identifies four life positions:

Life positions

I am OK and you are OK (+/+)	Mutual respect and equality between both parties. Relationship based on exchange, sharing and collaboration with the aim of achieving win-win results.
I am OK and you are not OK (+/-)	You are in a dominant position, having imposed your idea or demand on the other person without taking their needs or feelings into account. People who overvalue themselves and think that they are superior to others often behave in this way.
I am not OK and you are OK (-/+)	You have adopted a submissive position and accepted the other person's demand without expressing your opinion or your needs. This attitude often stems from a negative self-image and lack of self-esteem.
I am not OK and you are not OK (-/-)	The two parties are in total disagreement. The situation is a failure and no good can come of it. This can result from a lack of self-confidence, a lack of openness, a failure to listen and an absence of exchange between the two parties.

If you want to take both your needs and other people's needs into account, you need to aim for the "+/+" life position.

Openness before assertiveness

Being assertive also means having the courage to express yourself or to refuse, while remaining open and communicative. In order to achieve the right balance, you need to listen to and understand others and accept their position and needs before expressing your own. All too often, we fail to take the other person into account. As an example, we can consider a personal assistant who has been told not to let anyone disturb the manager and simply tells everyone that they are not available. The assistant does not make any effort to think about the importance or urgency of the call and the possible repercussions if the person is not able to reach the manager. Always be receptive to what the other person has to say and let them express their views.

Control your emotions

The emotions we feel every day are what make us human. However, when we are stressed they can overwhelm us, stop us from thinking straight and lead us to make mistakes. These emotions include anxiety over possible failure, disappointment caused by dissatisfaction with a situation, and anger, which can lead to intense frustration and even physical violence. When we let our emotions get the better of us, the situation can quickly spiral out of our control. The key to avoiding this is to develop a clearer understanding of what happens when we find ourselves in these situations.

To do this, analyse a recent conflictual situation and ask yourself: "What did I feel in this situation? Why did it make me angry, anxious or sad? Could I deal with this feeling? Did I express it, and how? How did I channel it?" These questions will allow you to understand and identify the cause of your emotions, which in turn will enable you to better control them.

For example, one night your boss asks you to stay for an extra hour to finalise a report, when you are supposed to be picking your children up from school. If you tend to give in to other people because you are afraid of disappointing them, this will probably make you feel a mixture of fear (you are afraid because your boss is an authority figure), frustration (you do not dare to express your needs) and sadness (you promised your children that you would be there). Analysing the situation, understanding why you feel the way that you do and learning how to channel your feelings will allow you to manage them better and, over time, to stand up for yourself.

Dare to speak up

Speaking up is usually easier said than done. We often use the other person's feelings as an excuse and avoid expressing ourselves, either because we are afraid of their reaction or because we are ashamed of what we want to say. We therefore opt to prioritise other people's needs and desires over our own. When one of your colleagues invites you to a seminar that does not interest you, instead of accepting out of politeness, be brave enough to listen to your feelings and turn them down. If your colleague takes offence, explain yourself calmly: "I don't think the seminar will be useful for me, because it has nothing to do with my work". Silence is not the answer, as it can leave the other person feeling frustrated or angry, which will damage your relationship with them. People will not know what you are feeling unless you tell them.

Effective communication

Understanding the need to express yourself is the first step. But how can you actually do this? Start by preparing what you are going to say based on real, tangible facts, which you can identify using the questions "Why? What? Where? When? How? How much?" This is a way of presenting the facts objectively and precisely, without relying on generalisations, personal opinions or accusations. Basing your argument on familiar information will boost your confidence and enable you to express yourself more easily, because it will be difficult to challenge what you are saying.

When expressing your feelings and needs, remain calm and communicate in a way that is appropriate for the situation. This will reduce the tension and make it easier for both sides to see eye to eye. Make sure that what you say is meaningful and formulate clear, concise demands, secure in the knowledge that this will make things better for both sides. During the conversation, let the other person express themselves and listen to their point of view. The examples below illustrate the approaches to avoid and the approaches to adopt in order to develop assertive behaviour.

Behaviour to avoid	Assertive behaviour
"Your work is never filed properly! You're so careless! We're all fed up of wasting time looking for your documents."	"Customer documents from the last two weeks haven't been filed. We're frustrated with this situation because it takes us too long to find the documents. Take some time to organise them this morning so that we can deal with the customers' requests as quickly as possible."
"I can't stay any later!"	"I'm aware that it's an important report, but I need to leave the office on time today because I've arranged to meet someone. If you'd told me earlier, I'd have been able to organise myself to fit it in. However, I could get here early tomorrow morning and finish it, if that works for you."

Behaviour to avoid	Assertive behaviour
"No, it's impossible!"	"We can't send the report this morning, because the printer isn't working and we're waiting for the repair man. However, I can email it while we're waiting."
"Whatever you want…"	"I hear what you're saying, but I'm not happy to deal with the file like that because I prefer to be honest with the customer."

Extra information

After you have listened to the other person and expressed your needs, end the conversation on a positive note by finding a compromise. Do not forget the key principles of assertiveness: empathy, standing up for yourself and respect for other people.

TOP TIPS

- **Neither passive nor aggressive.** Passivity may harm your wellbeing, but aggression risks making you an outcast in the office. Find the right balance: assertive behaviour involves affirming your needs, limits and opinions and making sure that they are respected, while remaining considerate and avoiding forcing them on others.
- **Get to know yourself better.** In order to assert yourself, you must be aware of your values, fears, emotions, needs and limits. After all, you cannot express them authentically if you do not know what they are!
- **Respect yourself and the other person.** You can only do this by stating your needs and feelings, as remaining silent about them will lead to frustration and stress. Respecting yourself also means knowing how to say no when the situation calls for it. Moreover, listening to and understanding the other person is not enough; you also need to make sure that your thoughts and words take their needs into account.

- **Be open to other people.** Before you express yourself, listen to the other person and stay receptive to what they feel and say in order to understand their position and find an effective compromise.

- **Express your emotions.** When you are embroiled in a difficult situation or conflict, identify, accept and channel the emotions you feel (anger, sadness, and so on) so that they do not overwhelm you. Use them positively by expressing them clearly to the other person so that they can understand the effect their words and actions have on you. If you lash out without explaining why, you will come across as intimidating, volatile or quick-tempered, but certainly not assertive.

- **Ask yourself the right questions.** This involves analysing the situation in order to understand it and deal with it more effectively. Ask yourself why it is bothering you; what needs you and the other person have; what kind of limit the other person has overstepped; and so on. Finally, do something constructive by asking "What solution could benefit everyone involved?"

- **Have the courage to say no.** Put things into

perspective: saying no to a request does not always have disastrous consequences. However, this does not mean that you should automatically turn down every request. Instead, you should analyse them and think about their consequences before making a decision: "What will the advantages and disadvantages be if I accept?"

- **End on a positive note.** As with Nonviolent Communication, it is important to end the conversation by coming to an agreement that is beneficial to both parties. Remember to thank the other person for listening to what you had to say.

ASSERTIVENESS IN NONVIOLENT COMMUNICATION

Assertiveness is one of the key communication skills in Nonviolent Communication, developed by the American psychologist Marshall Rosenberg (1934-2015). While assertiveness is an attitude, Nonviolent Communication is a communication technique. They are both based on authenticity, empathy and respect, and allow users to express themselves clearly and firmly, but

- **Think carefully about your words and actions.** If you want to assert yourself without coming across as aggressive, it is important to speak in a measured and respectful way and adapt your language to the situation. Pay attention to your voice too: do not speak too loudly and keep your tone neutral. Body language plays a vital role, so you should also watch your gestures (for example, pointing your finger at someone could be viewed as aggressive) and your facial expressions (avoid smirking). Stand up straight in order to project confidence and strength.
- **Do not give in.** If you want to develop assertive behaviour, stick to your guns and remain firm on your positions. If you give in, you risk losing face with the other person, who will not take your words seriously next time.
- **Take a step back.** Even if you are sure you know what your needs are at a given moment, you may change your mind when you think things over some more. Do not make impor-

tant decisions when you are feeling emotional.

<u>**TIP FOR EMPLOYEES**</u>

Standing up for yourself is not the same thing as being unpleasant or arrogant. When you are assertive, you make yourself seem confident and reassuring, which will improve your relationships with your colleagues and managers. Make sure that you stay true to yourself: if you are naturally reserved, there is no need to force yourself to impose yourself too much, as long as you do not feel that people are walking all over you. There is more than one way to be assertive, so do what feels right for your personality.

FAQS

WHAT IS ASSERTIVENESS?

Assertiveness is a behaviour and a communication technique based on respect for yourself and for other people. It is about standing up for yourself, stating your needs and opinions and defending your interests while also respecting those of the other person. An assertive person dares to say what they think with confidence and self-assurance, while remaining open and considerate. Developing this attitude will improve both your professional relationships and your personal wellbeing.

IN WHAT SITUATIONS CAN ASSERTIVENESS HELP ME?

Assertiveness can be useful in many situations: interactions with your manager, discussions with colleagues, meetings, disagreements, and so on. Assertiveness is also a significant element of Nonviolent Communication.

It is absolutely essential to be assertive with the right person. Asserting your opinion to someone who does not make the decisions will not be very helpful to you. For example, if your manager asks you to finish a project by the end of the week, but this is impossible because you do not have the material you need, objectively and calmly explaining this to your colleague will not get you anywhere. Instead, talk to your manager directly and explain why you will not be able to fulfil their request.

HOW CAN I BE ASSERTIVE WITHOUT COMING ACROSS AS AGGRESSIVE OR ARROGANT?

An assertive person is not aggressive or arrogant. While assertiveness is sometimes construed this way, this is simply due to a misinterpretation or miscommunication. Pay attention to your verbal and body language to make sure that you do not project a negative image of yourself. Asserting yourself firmly and confidently does not mean walking all over other people. If you find the right balance, you will be able to express your needs without frustrating or hurting the other person.

WHAT IS THE DIFFERENCE BETWEEN ASSERTIVENESS AND SELFISHNESS?

Saying what you think, and in particular saying no, does not mean that you are selfish. To avoid coming across as selfish, pay attention to how you express yourself: stay true to yourself, respect the other person and take both sides' needs into account in order to find a win-win solution.

HOW CAN I CHANGE MY BE-HAVIOUR TO BECOME MORE ASSERTIVE?

The first step is to take some time to get to know yourself better. Ask yourself the right questions: "Who am I? What do I like? What do I dislike? What are my skills and abilities? What are my weak points? What are my fears, values, limits and needs?"

Then, muster your courage and say what you think. Give your opinion calmly but firmly, making sure that you respect each person's interests and do not hurt the other person. Remember to remain open and receptive to the other person by listening to and considering their point of view.

WHAT IMPACT CAN ASSERTIVENESS HAVE ON MY PROFESSIONAL LIFE?

Assertiveness can transform your professional prospects by helping you to:

- develop healthy communication and professional relationships based on mutual respect;
- reduce sources of conflict and improve the general atmosphere;
- motivate your team by asserting yourself confidently and firmly;
- make your meetings more effective;
- easily negotiate and conclude deals and contracts;
- say no when you are snowed under with work;
- improve your personal and professional wellbeing.

OVER TO YOU

This exercise will allow you to evaluate how assertive you are and identify behaviours that you could improve. Think back to a time when you said yes to a request from a colleague or a manager when you really wanted to say no, and answer the questions below:

- What was the other person asking for? Was their request framed as "you need to" or "it would be good if"?
- What kind of limit did this cross for you?
- At that moment, what did you want and need? Did you express this?
- How did the situation make you feel? Did you mention these feelings?
- Were your values respected?
- Did you express everything you wanted to express? If so, what were the consequences of doing so? If not, why not?
- Did you identify and understand the other person's needs and values? If so, what were

they? If not, why not?

- Who made the final decision – you, them or both of you as a compromise? Why?
- Did you need and have the opportunity to negotiate?
- If the conversation ended badly, what approach could have you taken to conclude on a positive note?

DARING TO ASSERT YOURSELF

List different contexts in which you have had difficulty asserting yourself. This exercise will help you to get to know yourself better, analyse situations and put them into perspective, which will in turn give you the courage to state and stand up for your needs.

Exercise: daring to assert yourself

Situation			
My limits/my needs			
Possible negotiations			
Consequences if I say no			

FURTHER READING

BIBLIOGRAPHY

- Assertivité.net. (2013) *Définition et utilité de l'assertivité.* [Online]. [Accessed 26 September 2017]. Available from: <http://www.assertivite.net/definition-assertivite/>

- Corten, P. (2006) *Tuer le stress avant qu'il nous tue ! Manuel pratique de gestion du stress.* Brussels: Clinique du Stress CHU Brugman.

- Le Guernic, A. (No date) Les positions de vie. *AT.fr.* [Online]. [Accessed 26 September 2017]. Available from: <http://analysetransactionnelle.fr/les-concepts-de-base/les-positions-de-vie/>

- Tournebise, T. (2001) Assertivité. L'affirmation de soi dans le respect d'autrui. *Maieusthesie.com.* [Online]. [Accessed 26 September 2017]. Available from: <http://maieusthesie.com/nouveautes/article/assertivite.htm>

ADDITIONAL SOURCES

- Bronckart, V. (2017) *Nonviolent Communication at Work.* Trans. Probert, C. Brussels: Plurilingua Publishing.

- Paterson, R. J. (2002) *The Assertiveness Workbook: How to Express Your Ideas and Stand Up for Yourself at Work and in Relationships*. Oakland, California: New Harbinger Publications.

- Potts, C. and Potts, S. (2013) *Assertiveness: How to Be Strong in Every Situation*. Mankato, Minnesota: Capstone.

IMPROVE YOUR GENERAL KNOWLEDGE

IN A BLINK OF AN EYE !

www.50minutes.com

www.50minutes.com

Ebook EAN: 9782808000512

Paperback EAN: 9782808000529

Legal Deposit: D/2017/12603/453

Cover: © Primento

Digital conception by Primento, the digital partner of publishers.